Illustrations
of
Old Bideford

Volume Two

Peter Christie

Edward Gaskell *publishers*
DEVON

First published 2009
Edward Gaskell *publishers*
The Old Gazette Building
6 Grenville Street
Bideford
Devon
EX39 2EA

isbn (10) 1-906769-13-3
isbn (13) 978-1-906769-13-0

Illustrations of Old Bideford

Peter Christie

Typeset, printed and bound by
Lazarus Press
Caddsdown Business Park
Bideford
Devon
EX39 3DX
www.lazaruspress.com

Contents

Dedicated to
Roy Christie

Introduction

When I published *Illustrations of Old Bideford* last year I did say in my foreword that I had enough photographs to produce another volume - you are now holding that book. Once again I must thank all my fellow Bidefordians whose generosity in loaning me pictures from their family albums has made this second volume possible. As before I have tried to mix old and relatively newer photographs to give a balanced view of the many changes Bideford has gone through over the last 150 or so years. In preparing this volume for the printer I have realised I am well on my way to having enough illustrations for a third, and probably final, selection. Having said that I never cease to be amazed just how many photographs of our small market town and its people have been taken over the years. In the first volume I issued an invitation to anyone who had old pictures of Bideford who would like to share them to contact me at 9 Kenwith Road, Bideford EX39 3NW or ring Bideford 473577. Photographs in this book have been lent to me by the following people who retain the copyright.

Photographs have been lent to me by the following people who retain the copyright:

R.Ackland
E.Anderson
BAAC
J.Backway
J.Baker
H.Beer
Bideford Library
A.Blamey
G.Braddick
J.Bradley
J.Brownrigg
O.Chope
M.Cleaver
D.Clements
D.Cole
T.Cotter
M.Davey
T.Derrigan
V.Eastman

T.Farley
D.Gale
W.Grant
R.Hopkins
J.Jewell
M.Jewell
G.Jones
B.Lacey
L.Lane
R.Lloyd
R.Morris
North Devon Athenaeum
North Devon Journal
North Devon Museum Trust
G.de Rycke
A.Shute
J.Swain
T.Waters
J.Webb
P.Wells

Front Cover
This beautiful photograph shows a travelling fair on the Pill with its swing-boats and roundabouts. Kingsley's statue is already present so it post-dates 1906 but the clothes are definitely pre-First World War so I would date the shot to around 1910. Note the litter everywhere - who said things have just got worse in this respect?

The Bridge

Above: I have included this photograph, which dates from around the First World War, as it gives such a good view of both the Bridge and the 'Folly' on the right. Little is known about this building other than it apparently housed a school at the end of the nineteenth century and is now a domestic residence. The presence of sheep so close to the town might strike us as surprising today but at this date Bideford was much smaller than now.

Previous page: This aerial shot was taken in the 1930s and demonstrates the pivotal nature of the Bridge to the town. The Strand cinema which dates from 1939 hasn't been built, but clearly seen is Elliott's Garage which later became the Esso Garage. Kingsley Road (opened in 1927 at a cost of £29,000) still looks new whilst the Garden Theatre on the Pill has no houses bordering it.

Above: In the first volume I published various photographs of the collapse of the Bridge in 1968. Repairs took a long time and this photograph shows the roadway held up by a massive scaffolding structure which extended all along the river bank outside Tanton's Hotel.

Opposite: A crowded shot taken on June 3rd 1925 - following the widening of the Bridge by the Bridge Trust. To mark the occasion townspeople dressed as characters from Bideford's history and marched across the Bridge to a Pageant in the Sports Ground.

Above: Another photograph taken following the collapse of Bideford Bridge was taken in November 1969 and shows the final steps in the repair work as a small tracked piece of plant is lifted up by the massive crane. All Bidefordians breathed a sigh of relief when the long drawn out work was finally completed.

Opposite: Clearly taken from the tower of St.Mary's this panoramic shot, which dates from around 1900 shows all of the Bridge and manages, at the same time, to include all the buildings in East-the-Water between the railway station and Vinegar Hill. Chudleigh Fort is clearly seen not yet being obstructed by trees, whilst the industrial nature of the wharves at that side of the river is obvious.

Calls for a second bridge over the Torridge at Bideford go back as far as 1949 but it wasn't until May 1987 that a second crossing was finally opened. This shot shows construction going on in 1986. The bridge consumed 17,700 cubic metres of concrete and 2900 tonnes of steel reinforcement. The bridge was cast in sections which were then glued together in place, with permanent stressing cable then being installed and 'pulled together'. The whole structure cost £13.5 million.

On Sunday May 10 1987 the Torridge Bridge was opened up to Bidefordians to walk across - the first time it had been crossed by the local population. This photograph shows the huge crowds who availed themselves of the opportunity to make the crossing. On the day visitors were also allowed to walk through the bridge under the road - 'an unforgettable and probably unrepeatable experience' as it was termed at the time.

Shops

In the past the visit of the travelling fair to Bideford was a major event. Held for many years on the Pill it later transferred to the Riverbank car park. One of the great draws to young Bidefordians was Trigger's sweet stall seen here in its heyday probably some time before the war. Hilda Clements nee Trigger of Dolton is on the left and Beatie Little, who lived in Elm Grove in Bideford, is on the right.

The Chope family have been associated with Bideford for some 250 years and here we see the saddlery shop of Sidney Chope which was located in Buttgarden Street. This particular member of the family was Mayor for much of the First World War. The business was latterly run by Mr. Johns - whose work tools are now in the Burton Art Gallery and Museum.

Above: Hogg's Corner, named after the chemist who long occupied a shop here, was where New Road meets Bridge Street. The town council, who built the major part of the town hall in 1850-51 long coveted this site in order to allow expansion of their building - but it wasn't until the beginning of the twentieth century that they were finally able to purchase it - along with Pridham's offices and stables next door. Both were demolished and in 1906 the present-day town council chamber, Mayor's Parlour and Library were all opened on the site. Whilst the site was being prepared sixteen human skeletons were discovered and no-one could explain what they were doing there.

Opposite: The shop of Squire & Son stood at 12 High Street, on a site occupied today by Walter Henry's. The photograph was taken around 1904 and I assume it was specially posed given that the three large silver trophies on the left and the large ormolu clock on the right appear to be sitting outside on the pavement! A mosaic with the name of Squire worked into it still exists at the entrance to the shop today.

These buildings are long gone today - this being the site of the present Baptist church and forecourt in Mill Street. When this photograph was taken around 1900 T.M.Geen's shop and the Hill Garden Commercial Hotel and Restaurant occupied the space. I like the pot plants sitting rather precariously on the lintel over Geen's door.

H. I. MEREDITH,

Jronmonger and .
Sanitary Engineer,

18, HIGH STREET, BIDEFORD.

SOLE AGENT FOR NORTH DEVON FOR THE NOTED

Premier Air Gas Plant.

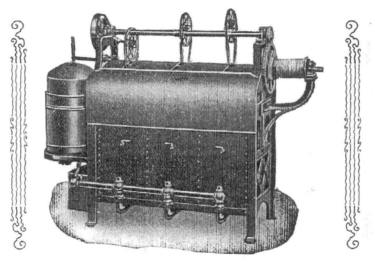

An Ideal System of Lighting

For Country Mansions, Bungalows, Houses, Churches, Chapels, Public
Buildings, Shops, Stations, Villages or Towns.

SIMPLE, SAFE, AND CHEAP.   NO MOTOR REQUIRED.
ESTIMATES FREE.
Telegrams, Meredith, Bideford.   Telephone 21.

This wonderful advertisement appeared in Wilson's 1913 'Commercial Almanack for
Bideford. The rather fearsome looking machine that could light your house was produced long before everyone was on mains gas and electricity as today. I wonder how
many of these plants were actually sold and installed?

Frayne's grocery and butcher's shop in the High Street was certainly busy when this photograph was taken. I suspect it shows a Christmas queue sometime in the late 1940s/early 1950s. The shop has gone through several changes ending up split into a second-hand goods shop on the left and a record/bookshop I ran on the right. Since then the shop frontages have been removed and the whole building converted to flats.

Above: This cheerful looking group of ladies in their immaculate white work tops were the employees of the Bideford branch of Boots pictured in 1945. Unfortunately I can only supply the name of the two on the extreme right - Betty Braund and Dorothy Grant. Since this was taken, of course, the shop frontage behind them has been greatly altered - and the shop itself has migrated several times since then.

Overleaf: Not really a 'shop' I know but this open air exhibition of caravans on the Pill in the late 1950s or early 1960s shows an interesting view of the town. Bath House, the white building in the centre, is now owned and run by Devon County Council and the 'Blues,' in the building on the left, are still there as is the Repository in Rope Walk. The stone built buildings on the right have disappeared and been replaced by the Post Office sorting yard area.

This tiny shop has long disappeared. It stood between the present-day Angling Club and a small terrace of houses owned by the Bridge Trust at the top of Honestone Street. Such small shoe repair shops were common in the past but have virtually disappeared now. The two men in the photograph, which dates from around 1920, are, on the left, Mr. Tanton and on the right Tom Cotter.

Above: This small shop at 3-4 Meddon Street was that of J.T.Mitchell, a decorator. The window is decorated with ribbons used to create a Union Jack on the occasion of George VI's coronation. Today it houses Blackwell's Pasties.

Opposite: For many years Harry Shute (holding up the card in the photograph) ran a successful shoe shop in Grenville Street but as with everyone he eventually reached retirement age and this picture was taken in April 1969 on the very day he retired - I must say he doesn't look too upset about it! I later ran the shop for a decade as a secondhand book and record business.

Bideford's Pannier Market can trace its origins back definitely to 1574 when the town's charter was granted by Elizabeth I - though it was almost certainly being held before then on an ad hoc basis. Located originally at the bottom of the High Street it moved in the seventeenth century to its present site but seems to have been a rather ramshackle affair. At this date it was still controlled by the Lord of the Manor but in 1881 the town council purchased it from him and built what is today's building. This shot shows the interior in 1990.

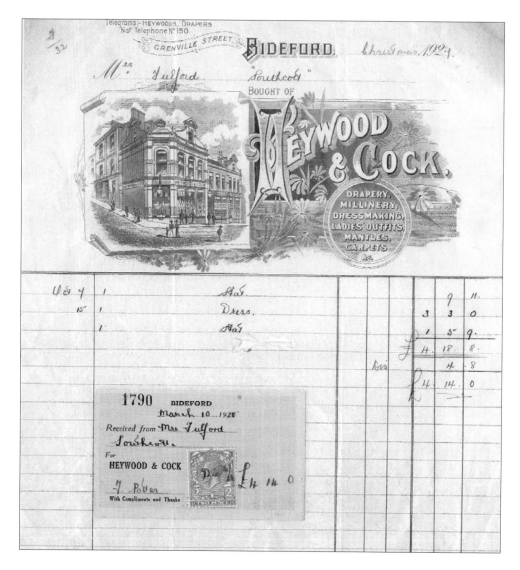

Above: Ornamental billheads acted as both a receipt and an attractive advertisement for the businesses that produced them.

Previous page: George Boyles Ltd. was a family run firm selling men's and women's clothing and soft furnishings which had traded in Bideford for some 150 years. In January 1981 the shop was sold by its owner George Durant and this photograph was taken then. The original business started in Appledore when the first George Boyle (Mr.Durant's great grandfather) took over a women's drapery store from his aunt in Market Street. He later moved near to the Market in Bideford and then around 1850 to the High Street in what is today The Card Box before finally moving to the shop complex on the corner of Allhalland and High Street.

The ornamental bill heads for both Walter H. Chope and Heywood & Cock (see previous page) followed the usual convention of showing human figures as very small - in order to emphasise the size of their shop fronts.

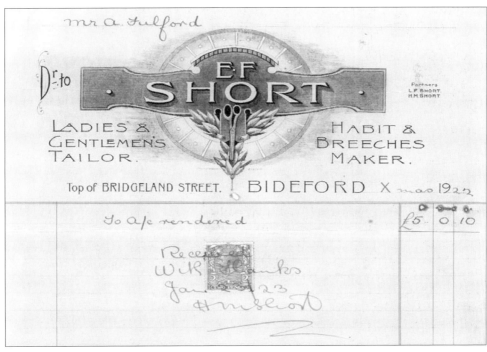

This photograph dates from the early 1970s and shows the 'Rose Bird' shop in Mill Street - but look at the shops beyond it which have all changed. 'Bazaar' and 'Cafecino' have replaced the shops then present - but 'Taylor Bros' on the right of the shot is still there - one of the longer surviving family businesses in the town.

Buildings

This photograph is not easily recognisable today as so many changes have occurred to the buildings. The ceremonial archway bears the mottoes 'God Save the Queen' and 'Long May She Reign' which probably dates it to the year of Victoria's Diamond Jubilee in 1897 The site is the junction of North Road and Chingswell Street. The buildings in the background were replaced by Yeo's large drapery store - still present today as a pet shop.

This very unusual view of Bideford Quay, which seems to have been taken from the upper windows of the Talbot Inn in High Street, dates from around 1900. The still new trees are small and, today, who would casually stand in the road gossiping like the people here?

The Three Tuns on the Quay was once Sir Bevil Grenville's town house but was extensively rebuilt and now houses the Freebird shop. It was one of four adjoining public houses that once lined the Quay - today only the King's Arms survives. The poster overleaf shows it being offered for sale in 1822. At this date it contained a 'Brewhouse' as all beer was brewed on the premises - a common set-up in those days.

BIDEFORD.

To be Sold

BY AUCTION,

The Fee-simple and Inheritance of

ALL that well-accustomed

PUBLIC HOUSE

known by the Name of

The Three Tuns,

SITUATED

ON THE QUAY

in the Town of Bideford,

Now in the Possession of Robert Ley.

The Premises comprise a good Dwelling House, Brewhouse, and other convenient Offices, with a spacious Corn Loft adjoining, and are conveniently situate for Business.

For Selling the same a Survey will be held at the said Public House on Thursday the 7th day of November next, at 4 o'clock in the afternoon.

For viewing the Premises apply to the Tenant, and for further Particulars to Mr. CHARLES ROBERTS, Solicitor, Barnstaple.

Dated Oct. 24th, 1822.

Syle, Printer, Barnstaple.

This odd looking building once stood on the Quay outside today's Post Office - if you cannot place it look at the Art School on the right. It was known as the Manor House but I am unaware of any manorial link. Notice the lifebelt hanging on the wall in between the house fronts. The building was eventually demolished leaving enough room in front of the Post Office to allow for a small parking area to be laid out.

This picture from around 1890 shows construction going on of two bay-fronted houses in the High Street which still remain today. The house next to these was about to be demolished and replaced with the present-day Methodist chapel. Notice the boy in his oversized 'Eton' collar carrying milk cans.

If you had been in Allhalland Street in 1900 you would have seen this scene. The very distinctive upper windows of the building in the centre are still there but the shop front is completely changed.

"Mate"

Bideford High Street in 1904 – without a car in sight even though they had reached the town by this date. The shop windows may have changed and all the sunblinds have disappeared but it is surprising, perhaps, to see how little about the buildings has actually altered.

Readers may recognise Kingsley Terrace on the brow of the hill but how many remember the house in the foreground? It appears to be a rare example of a Devon long-house but even so it was cleared away in the early 1970s when the industrial yard that now occupies the site was extended.

This wonderfully atmospheric shot would be hard to place for even the eldest Bidefordian. The only clue as to where it was is the small, just visible, chapel. Both it and the houses have now gone but they used to stand at Old Town, the chapel being used for burial services at the graveyard that still occupies the site today. The photograph dates from around 1890-1900.

In 1925 the Bideford Hospital in Abbotsham Road was opened to huge acclaim but this photograph shows the laying of the foundation stone some time before. The hospital replaced the old one in Meddon Street which went on to become the town's maternity hospital and then a care home for the elderly.

This was the old hospital in Meddon Street referred to on the previous page when its main entrance was straight off of the pavement at the front. This has long been closed up - and today the building is set for demolition and replacement with flats and houses.

I was really pleased to come across this photograph which shows Willet Street as it is the only old shot I know of this small road. The wall on the left surrounded a large private garden at this date whilst the old Garden Theatre has yet to be built at the end of the road. The date of the shot is probably around 1890-1900.

West Bank School was founded in 1896 at Lansdowne Terrace and following rapid growth it moved into these handsome buildings on Belvoir Road. In 1955 the entire school moved to Sidmouth and its Bideford buildings were taken over by Grenville College which, in 2008, announced it was amalgamating with Edgehill College to form Kingsley College. Whether these buildings will continue in use as a school is uncertain.

Edgehill Girls' College, Bideford. — The Gymnasium.

1907.5

This photograph with its inscription is self-explanatory. One might consider these clothes as not really being suited to strenuous exercise but in the years before the First World War, when this posed shot was taken, such uniforms would have been seen as quite liberating!

In 1884 Edgehill College was opened by the Bible Christians and it grew steadily over the years. Unfortunately a fire broke out in 1920 and completely destroyed the buildings. The blackened ruins are shown in this striking photograph.

This famously was the smallest shop in Bideford. Situated in Allhalland Street it still stands but is now a private house or rather the entrance hall to a house. For many years it was a confectionery shop selling ice cream and sweets.

This rare aerial shot shows the old Barton farm at East-the-Water. The farm was engulfed by new housing estates and lost its outbuildings but the central farmhouse became The Barton public house - which in its turn was demolished several years ago to be replaced by a small 'mews' style development of housing.

This was Boyle's cycle shop on the corner of Bridge and Allhalland Street shortly before its demolition in the late 1960s. This and the neighbouring building were removed leaving the old alleyway just visible on the right of this photograph. The alley-way still exists whilst the site of the buildings now provides the entrance to the car park.

'Ordinary' houses in 'ordinary' streets are rarely photographed but these were recorded in 1961 to illustrate a Bideford borough council guide to services – which included council-built houses such as these at the Grenville Estate Clovelly Road.

I have included these two shots of Mill Street to show how a variety of small changes
have altered the street scene in so much of Bideford. In the first Ford & Spry and a
Health Food store (with, rather bizarrely, Army recruitment posters in the window)
are present whilst in the second the fronts have been knocked through prior to their
rebuilding some 40 years ago. Nicklin's shop later became a butcher's run by Terry
Derrigan and today houses Getset Designs.

Anyone visiting the town finds it hard to believe that this building once existed. It was Island House which stood just in front of Victoria Terrace and provided a very sharp bend for motorists coming down Honestone Street. It was a public house in the seventeenth century though it ended its days as a Salvation Army 'Citadel'. The phone box shown in the picture was Bideford's first such one - and I had it listed as an ancient monument some 25 years ago.

Above: The old Church Junior School was built at the corner of Honestone and High Street in 1845 but by the 1970s was clearly unsuitable as a modern education facility - and in 1975 it was closed. Its replacement was St.Mary's Primary School in Chanters Road. The photograph shows the new school under construction in February 1975 - with opening scheduled for April of that year.

Overleaf: The house and railings on the right are still here but all those buildings opposite were demolished in the early 1970s. Note the 'bridge' into one of them and the drop from the pavement down to their ground floors. Kipling mentions these shops in his *Stalky & Co* as places from which he purchased small antiques when attending the United Services College at Westward Ho!

In the 1960s the town council undertook a clearance of old properties deemed sub-standard and amongst the areas cleared was New Street as shown in this photograph. It is this area that is pictured in the photograph on p.156 when the tightly knit community was still in existence.

The plaque clearly sites and dates this photograph - Bideford in April 1979. It shows the Lord Lieutenant of Devon Field Marshal Sir Richard Hull unveiling a commemorative plaque recording the opening of a new extension at Bideford College some 4 years after it first opened. Standing at the right is John Dare the headmaster whilst between them is Ted Pinney chair of Devon's Education Committee.

Bidefordians will instantly recognise the statue of Charles Kingsley but how many can recall when the town's Army Cadets cleaned him? The date was November 1983 and the Cadets undertook the job as part of a community project designed to win them their proficiency badges. They went on to clean the Pine-Coffin bust in the garden at the end of the Bridge as well.

Just to show that photographs do not have to be old to be of interest I have included this one from August 2003 which shows the old workshops and garages that stood opposite Hyfield Place off of Meddon Street. Since this shot was taken the buildings beyond the satellite dish have all been demolished and replaced by new housing.

Above: In 1974 plans were announced to build a huge new housing estate at Londonderry Farm on the outskirts of town. Needless to say there were large scale protests against the idea with objectors pointing out problems with drainage and traffic flows in the area - but by September 1981 when this photograph was taken building had commenced. The picture shows Jim Needs, chairman of Torridge district council, cutting the ribbon to declare the site officially open - with councillor Pam Paddon (in hat) looking on. The price of the houses at that date? - £22,000 for a 2 bedroom semi-detached bungalow rising to £33,500 for a 4 bed detached house.

Overleaf: When the railway in Bideford was closed the large area of the goods yard on the riverbank was left derelict. After many years of indecision Torridge district council eventually bought the site and in April 1981 began building new flats for old people there - at a cost of £1.5 million. The photograph, which dates from December 1981 shows construction going on.

Industry

This wonderful shot shows the Bideford Gas Works at East-the-Water sometime around 1900. The Bideford Gas Company was first set up in December 1835 with 60 shareholders and a Mr.Partridge as its manager and within a short time many householders were utilising this new source of energy. The size of the two gasometers in this photograph can be appreciated by looking at the two men standing on the walkways. The site is still industrial today though the old 'town gas' (derived from coke) has long been replaced by 'natural gas.'

The well-designed looking mobile knife and cutlery sharpening workshop was pictured in 1975 and you can clearly see the Bideford connection. It had been acquired by Preston Isaac of Chittlehampton who was 'assembling a museum' of such intriguing historic items.

Above: This astonishingly ornate building, for a factory, with the manager's house tacked on, was one of the collar works in Bideford. The town became a major centre for the production of collars and shirts following the establishment of the first small undertaking at Old Town in May 1871 which later moved to New Street. In November 1882 Vincent & Duncan, owners of the business, bought this 'genteel detached residence' and converted it into their new factory.

Overleaf: This section of a map surveyed in 1886 shows the site of the factory which today is covered by houses around Northview Avenue.

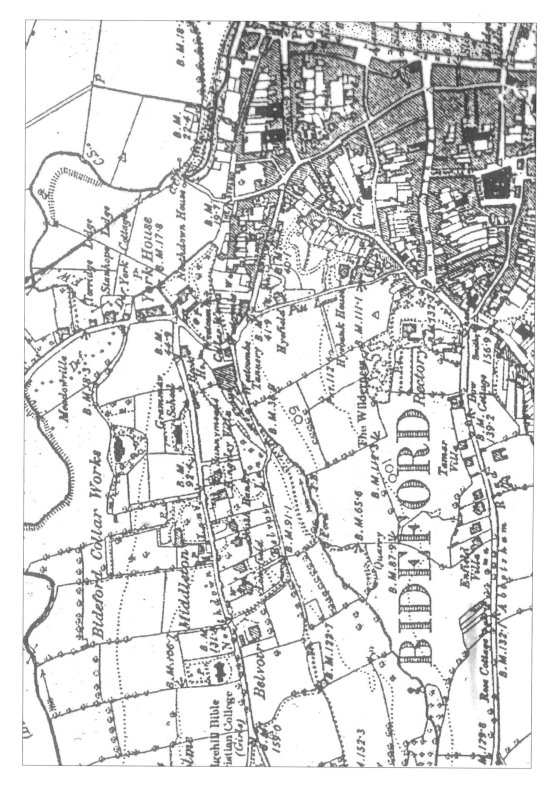

These cheerful looking men (and baby) were workers at Braddick's upholstery works at East-the-Water snapped sometime before World War One. Workplace shots are relatively rare and very few look as light-hearted as this one.

This view of the wharves at East-the-Water with the massive warehouses and sailing ships only dates from 1935 but could actually have been from anytime before the 1970s . Today it is vastly changed with a fairly soul-less car park now occupying most of the area.

Above: Westcombe Depot pictured in the 1930s. At this period it was used as the engineering workshop of Heard Brothers - hence the ramp up to the first storey. The building still exists today being used by Torridge district council - although there are plans to move its operations elsewhere and replace the building with housing.

Overleaf: Bartlett's timber firm was a large undertaking at the start of the twentieth century which was based where today's Jewsons is located at East-the-Water. This picture shows a group of their workers sitting outside the building housing the industrial bandsaw. Lots of moustaches - and two beards, one of them huge - are on display with lots of work caps and hobnails on the boots. Note the presence of a cat and a dog who were probably working animals used to combat vermin.

Bideford Pool by the Bridge used to be a focal point for salmon netsmen but is no longer used. In 1974 when this photograph was taken, however, local fishermen still fished it - and the picture shows brothers Leslie and Michael Barnes mending their nets outside of Tanton's Hotel ready for the opening of the fishing season on April 1st of that year.

Above: When this photograph first appeared in the *Journal* it was titled 'Music for the Pope'. It shows Steven Telford (left) and Mark Landolfi preparing an electronic organ at Wyvern Organs in Bideford in August 1979 which was to accompany Pope John Paul II on a tour of Ireland. An intriguing and rather specialised export from Bideford - to say the least.

Overleaf: Elsewhere in this book are pictures of the outdoor celebrations staged to mark the coronation of George VI in 1937. This 'indoor' one shows the women employed at the glove factory at the same time. This factory was in Silver Street the building housing it being an old Bible Christian chapel erected in 1844. It was demolished in April 2004 and a small housing development now occupies the site.

Above: This curious vehicle was used at the Rola factory which was an undertaking producing secret equipment for the RAF which had moved out of London to Bideford to escape bombing in the Second World War. It eventually returned to London sometime after the war.

Opposite: In the 50s and 60s local traders got together to put on various industrial exhibitions - usually in the Sports Ground. This shows the interior of one of the marquees with Braddick's display dominating the tent. The cane chairs, early fridges, old fashioned prams and radios all give it a wonderfully period feel.

North Devon workers do not have a history of industrial militancy but occasionally strikes were reported in the *Journal*. In February 1967 MPJ Gauge & Tool Co in Bideford sacked 13 of its 180 workers without notice - and the rest of the men immediately downed tools and walked out. The photograph taken in Jubilee Square shows the factory's draughtsmen handing leaflets out in support of their position.

This resplendent looking gentleman was Windsor postman Fred Fuzzens pictured in a nineteenth century postman's uniform. In 1975 he walked around Bideford and the local area literally following in the footsteps of his great hero Edward Capern. This man was Bideford's 'Postman Poet' who, although self-taught, went on to have best-selling books which were read by Charles Dickens and the Duke of Wellington and who was championed by Charles Kingsley.

If you were living in Bideford in the 1970s you will probably remember this gentleman. He was Mark Mountjoy and he had been the town's street cleaner from 1969. Over the years Mark had used discarded toys to decorate his barrow - and he became a much loved and photographed town 'character'. He is shown here in August 1980 on his retirement day.

Transport

This Thornycroft lorry looks as solid as a tank. The solid tyres, massive carbide lamps and heavy steel bodywork all give the impression of strength but look at the window with its split screen and no side panels! The driver is still wearing leather buskins which I think of as from horse wagon days. The lorry belonged to Goaman & Sons who were wholesale grocers based in Buttgarden Street. I would date the shot to around 1915-20.

Above: This strangely empty photograph of the Quay dates from around 1900 and shows the then newly planted double row of trees in a town landscape bereft of cars and people. The mix of sailing craft and steam driven vessels is clearly illustrated and I would guess the photographer had risen very early one Sunday to secure this shot.

Opposite: This close-up of two 'steamers' shows one unidentified boat plus the *Advance* of Barnstaple with a couple of crew members aboard. Such small vessels carried out a variety of jobs and were common on the Torridge up until the Second World War. Given the width of the Quay I would date this particular shot to around 1910. The chains on the Quay were to stop vehicles and pedestrians toppling over the edge into the river - a sadly common occurrence in the past.

A very atmospheric picture dating from 1927 showing Clarence Wharf at East-the-Water. The four vessels in the photograph are; alongside the quay the *Result* (with the crane) and an unidentified sailing barge whilst the large steamer moored in the river is either the *Stanley Force* or the *Snowflake*. The small sailing vessel alongside the latter is unidentified.

The rather complicated history of the *Kathleen & May* has been set out elsewhere but this fine shot dates from September 1970 when she was in dry dock at Bideford Shipyard. She had been drawn up to allow her condition below the water line to be surveyed. The Duke of Westminster's Maritime Trust had just acquired her after she had lain for 3 years on the mud banks off of Appledore.

Above: In the first volume of old photographs of Bideford I published I included one of the very atmospheric shots taken by Tom Farley who recorded every boat arriving in Bideford in the middle years of the 1950s. This is another of Tom's shots and shows a sailing vessel being unloaded by the old grab crane with a sea going crane behind the vessel - which is possibly the *Emily Barratt* or *Mary Stewart*.

Opposite: The last survival of Bideford's proud shipbuilding past was the yard of Bideford Shipbuilders 1973 Ltd. at Bank End. Long gone the site now houses the offices of Torridge District Council but in April 1974 the yard had just completed constructing this 72' Clyde-class lifeboat for the Royal National Lifeboat Institution - which by co-incidence was celebrating its 150th anniversary in that year. Following trials the vessel went to be stationed at Clovelly.

The year 1972 was marked by a national dockworkers' strike which closed most national ports. Bideford, however, having non-unionised stevedores, suddenly became attractive to ships trying to unload their cargoes and this photograph from July 1972 shows the 600 ton m.v. Hanni-Lene from Germany unloading a cargo of bulk grain on the Quay - a strike-breaking initiative which didn't go down too well with local trade unionists in the town.

This striking photograph shows the m.v.*Prince Ivanhoe*, owned by Waverley Excursions Ltd., leaving Bideford carrying 850 day trippers to Lundy in June 1981. It looks a perfect scene but sadly the vessel hit very bad weather and hundreds were ill - yet when they finally arrived at the island the sky cleared and they had a sun filled day to make up for the crossing.

This photograph is self-explanatory. It shows Hobart Braddick posing proudly by his new lorry on the Pill in 1924. Note the then new-fangled pneumatic tyres, the flat windscreen and hand-operated horn. No side windows, of course, but drivers were hardy back then.

These two photographs provide a good panoramic 'sweep' across the Bideford railway forecourt around 1900. The group of carriages is probably waiting for passengers to alight from the train at the platform. The small signal box allows the viewer to fix the position of the photographers - and note the horse-drawn wagon of Pridham & Son who were a major player in the coaching and wagon trade of Bideford and district through the nineteenth century.

Above: In 1974 the old railway bridge over Torrington Street, East-the-Water was found to be so low as to be restricting the entrance of lorries to the industrial units at Kynochs - so British Rail agreed to the raising of the whole structure by 4 feet. A huge crane arrived on site and bodily lifted the whole thing up the required distance as shown in the photograph.

Opposite: In the first volume of this series I printed a photograph of Bideford railway station being demolished in September 1968. Since then another series of such photographs has turned up including this very striking one. It shows the canopy on the western platform being removed - with debris casually scattered across the track. The surviving canopy on the platform opposite is yet to be removed - leaving the building we still see on the site today. I wonder if the station will ever be re-opened for rail traffic?

Above: This was the same scene as the previous page photographed from a different angle some eleven years later. The removal of the canopy exposed a rather utilitarian structure and though a single track still remains it was soon to disappear altogether - to eventually be replaced by the Tarka Trail.

Opposite: Horse-drawn coaches rapidly gave way to motor vehicles such as this - a local bus pictured on the Quay around 1910-15. The split windscreen and absence of any other windows must have made for an invigorating journey if nothing else. Certainly the solid tyres suggest it wouldn't have been very comfortable. I like the little bugle horn by the steering wheel.

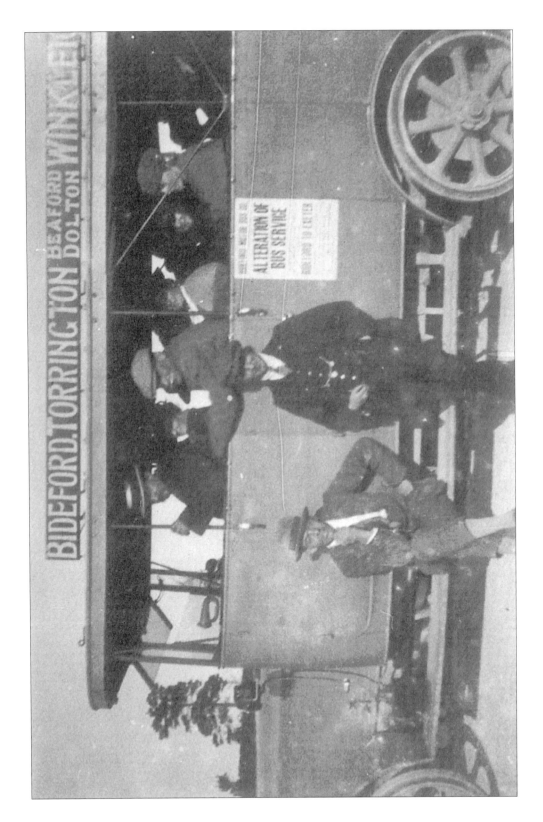

91

Above: Cars began to appear in Bideford around 1900 and soon grew in popularity - so much so that in 1910 the town council erected signs - featuring red paint on a white background - at the six major entrances to the town bearing a plea to drivers to slow down. This odd photograph records one of these very early vehicles at the top of Bridge Street with the Pannier Market behind. I say odd as clearly the car is not moving and one wonders why this incredibly steep part of the hill was chosen for the picture. As to the car itself note the solid tyres, bodywork which echoes that of horse-drawn carriages - and the carbide lamp hanging rather loosely on the back. The number plate seems to be LN 3386.

Opposite: Taken outside Tanton's Hotel this picture shows a holiday group in their best clothes about to set out on a trip - possibly to Clovelly - sometime before the First World War. The all-female group of passengers suggests this might be a Church group or ladies from one of Bideford's several collar and shirt factories.

These two photographs show 'Sentinel' steam lorries belonging to the Devon Trading Co. which was sited at the eastern end of the Bridge. Both shots were taken at the Sentinel Works in Shrewsbury on the day the lorries were dispatched to Bideford. The lorry with solid tyres (a 15 tonner) is pre-1930 whilst the other with pneumatic tyres (a 10 tonner) is post-1930.

This spectacular crash of a traction engine occurred at the bottom of Torridge Hill around 1924. The vehicle belonged to I.Baker & Son whose builder's yard was located at the eastern end of the Bridge. I am unsure how the heavy engine was righted but certainly the gentleman in the picture, who I assume was the driver, looks fairly disconsolate.

All these early motorcycles were collected together in Jubilee Square sometime before the First World War. I can only assume this is a meeting of the Bideford motorcycle club just prior to them setting out on a club outing. The open fronted, leather backed side-car looks rather chilly - perhaps explaining why there is no passenger in it!

On p.86 we saw an early vehicle owned by Braddick's - clearly the business flourished as some years later they could afford to upgrade to this splendid, and undoubtedly less chilly, vehicle. Note the double digit telephone number and the variety of goods the firm was selling by this date. The photograph was taken on the river bank by the entrance to the Park probably in the early 1930s.

This fine pair of horses with their 'horse brasses' prominently on display, were photographed crossing the Bridge in the 1930s. The driver, on the left, was James Harris whilst his passenger was Alfred Found. Modern readers may not realise just how common a sight this would have been at that date - cars were becoming commoner but horses were still important to the transport system.

Above: This shot was taken on Clarence Wharf, East-the-Water in the 1950s and shows Charlie Wrey driving a 'work horse' of those years - the 5 ton Bedford. Mr.Wrey was engaged in clearing mud from the berth at the Wharf which was as much a problem at that date as it is now. The massive warehouse in the background shows just how important this area was to the port.

Overleaf: I haven't included many unlocated photographs in my various books but I am assured this is a local cyclist from around 1890. His racy-looking costume clearly complemented his bicycle but note the solid tyres, carbide lamp and extravagantly sprung saddle and how streamlined the frame of the machine looks. Personally I wouldn't want to try this - but the owner looks very proud of it.

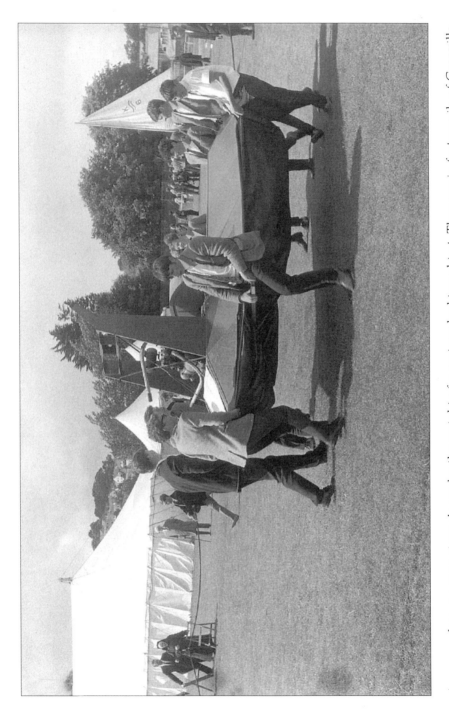

A group of young men struggle under the weight of a curious looking object. They are in fact pupils of Grenville College in Bideford bringing their school-built Mark III hovercraft to the town's Trade Exhibition in June 1968. Unfortunately the craft didn't get off the ground 'due to technical trouble'. Do any schools build such exciting craft now I wonder?

The Council

In 1925 the Bideford Rotary Club contacted its counterpart in Biddeford, Maine, USA and began a link that three years later saw the then Mayor of Bideford Alderman W.T.Goaman and his daughter, the Mayoress, visit Biddeford. The next year the Mayor of Biddeford Dr. George Precourt and his wife returned the visit. They were welcomed at the town hall as shown in this photograph which dates from May 1929 and shows councillor W.H. Fulford, the then town Mayor, and his American guests standing on the steps to the building. The high point of the visit was the opening by Dr. Precourt of a new 'parking ground' on the Pill which had been constructed at a cost of £950. Biddeford was named in 1616 by Richard Vine an early settler from Bideford - whose statue now stands in Biddeford.

This impressive group of police, soldiers and nurses plus townspeople gathered outside the Town Hall in May 1937 to hear the town clerk proclaim the crowning of George VI following the abdication of Edward VIII.

In 1605 John Andrew, a rich merchant of Bideford, died and in his will he left some land the rent from which was to be used by his trustees to help the poor of the town. The land became the playing fields next to Bideford College and the trustees are still distributing the money. This photograph from January 1958 shows the Mayor of the day councillor E.D.Williams in the Mayor's Parlour distributing bread (in lieu of money) to a few of the recipients that year. The lady shaking hands with the Mayor is Mrs.M.Steer.

Above: Bideford's existence as an agricultural market town has long gone but in the past the town had its own livestock market. Up until the last years of the nineteenth century animals seem to have been sold in the streets around the Pannier Market but the council then purchased a site in Honestone Street This photograph was probably taken around 1920. Note the sheep penned in on the right whilst the men leaning against the pens seem to be local farmers in wet weather clothing.

Overleaf: This photograph is looking towards the other direction and seems to show the opening ceremony - note the houses in the background which still exist today.

Following the privations of the war years the coronation of Queen Elizabeth II in June 1953 saw a huge outpouring of pride and hope for the future across the country - and here in Bideford the occasion was celebrated with an 'Elizabethan Fair' held in the Sports Ground on the afternoon of the Coronation. The Mayor of the day C.A.Grant opened the festivities from a temporary stage - ending his speech with a call to the crowd to 'make merry together'.

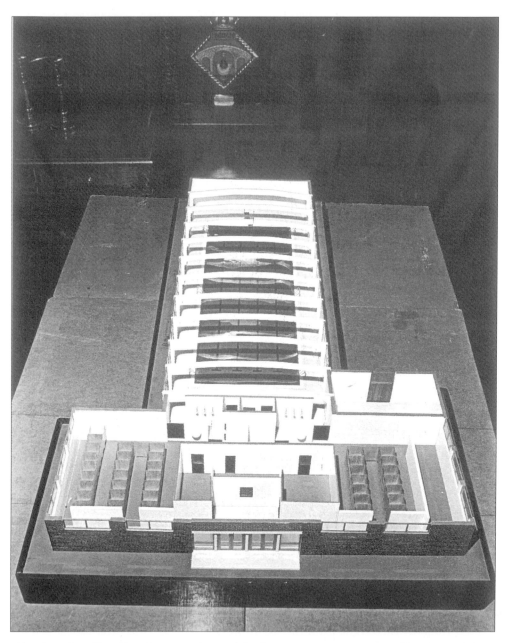

The fact that Torridge District Council built a swimming pool at Northam rather than Bideford left a lot of townspeople fuming - but at one time the town had the chance to build a pool here but didn't take it. In February 1964 the old borough council voted to build a 25 metre long pool at a cost of £60,000 in Victoria Park. A model was constructed and this photograph records it. At the time councillor Ethelwynne Brown declared the pool as more suited 'to the luxury of Beverly Hills' than to Bideford! Unfortunately a shortage of funds saw the plan put on the shelf - until it was quietly forgotten about which, sadly, is the fate of many council 'initiatives'.

Above: Not strictly a 'council' related shot but one that records the exercise of democracy. In October 1964 a General Election was held and the residents of Lundy voted along with every one else. This shot shows the 6 votes cast (out of the island's then 15 residents) being brought ashore from the m.v. Lundy Gannet in order to be counted. It was laconically recorded at the time that 'no canvassers bother the island.'

Overleaf: Up until 1974 when local government was re-organised and Bideford lost its self-governing borough status it was possible for the council to award the 'Freedom of the Borough' to notable townspeople. In October 1973, just before Torridge District Council took over the running of Bideford, this honour was awarded to Miss Phyllis Durant. In this photograph we see the presentation of an illuminated scroll by Mayor Ted Hill in the town council chamber. The badges being worn by four of the other people in the picture are those given to ex-Mayors to record their year in office.

Bideford as a town has always marked Remembrance Day. The event is led by the Mayor and today the wreath laying takes place both at Chudleigh Fort and in Victoria Park. This photograph, from November 1979, shows the Mayor about to lay the first wreath outside the Bideford Red's Club House next to the Post Office. Today the numbers attending this event are in the hundreds unlike the rather small crowd in this photograph.

Wartime

This bizarre photograph dates from September 1938 and shows Commander A.F.Reynolds the ex-Royal Navy Devon County Air Raid Precautions Instructor (in the centre) directing a training operation at the Westcombe Depot. The other gentleman in the hat is H.V.Cope the Area ARP Organiser for North Devon. The men are dressed in the strange costumes so that they could tackle a mustard gas attack. The photograph seems to have been taken as part of a publicity drive to obtain more recruits to the ARP as North Devon had only attracted 1453 volunteers from a target of 2500

What a fine selection of facial hair on display in this carefully posed photograph showing the band of the 'B' Company of the Bideford Volunteer Battalion of the Devonshire Regiment. I especially like the mutton chop whiskers of the Band Master and the little boy on the right who is proudly holding his triangle. The gentleman on the left at the end of the middle row is William Grant.

Sadly this photograph is undated though I would guess it is around 1890 - Hogg's chemist shop is still at the end of the Bridge and this didn't disappear until the opening of the twentieth century. It shows the band of the Bideford Volunteer Battalion of the Devonshire Regiment marching across the Bridge accompanied by fascinated young boys. I'm not sure who the soldier pushing the cycle is and why he is at the head of the group. Could he have been an officer who opted for this modern form of transport in preference to a horse?

This is a very rare shot of Bideford Quay during the early years of the Second World War showing the 'dragon's teeth' tank obstacles and festoons of barbed wire placed there to prevent the Nazis invading from the river. The obstacles were put in position by the town council who later removed them when their utility was judged to be over.

BOROUGH OF BIDEFORD

IMPORTANT !!

Water Supply

The presence of comparatively large numbers of evacuated children, and others, in the Borough necessitate that particular care should be exercised in the consumption of water, which should now be used for domestic purposes only.

Domestic purposes do not include watering lawns or gardens. The use of hose for cleaning motor cars is strictly forbidden.

Consumers are reminded that heavy penalties are provided for permitting water to be wasted or improperly used. As the water service is vital for all inhabitants, a loyal observance of the above request is expected.

By order of the Town Council,

F. C. BACKWAY,

Town Clerk.

24th June, 1940.

PEARSE & SON, Printers, BIDEFORD.

This small handbill is a rare survival of Second World War ephemera. Printed in small numbers to meet a local need I suspect this copy is unique. The message will be strangely familiar to those who can recall the great drought of 1976 - although it was natural conditions then rather than evacuee children who were responsible for the shortage of water.

This detachment of the Bideford Home Guard were photographed on exercise somewhere locally - possibly in Abbotsham Road or at Westward Ho! Names, in as far as they are known are, Back row (left to right); ?, ?, Slim Youngs, ?, Dick Cade, Freddie Clements (holding a sten gun), ?, ?, Ted Webb, ?, ?. Front row; ?, ?, ?, Frank Clark (the very young looking soldier), ?, ?, Dick Halbert (in glasses), ?, Charlie Brough, ?, ?, ?, ?.

5th (Bideford) Bn. Devon Home Guard.
No. 4 Sec. "C" Coy.—1941.

BACK ROW.—F. Ebsworthy, W. H. Stevens. C. Ridd. A. E. Reece. C. F. J. Southcott. E. Glover.
S. Branch. W. P. Vaughan.

FRONT ROW.—J. Blackmore. Sergt. H. Shute. Major J. H. Lowther (O.C. "C" Coy.). Lt. W. J. Woolf.
Cpl. H. Jeffery.

Leslie Cobb, Bideford.

This self-explanatory photograph was taken under the railway bridge at East-the-Water a year after the Home Guard had been embodied. Three of the men display ribbons on their chest indicating previous military service.

The Mayor in this photograph, taken on the Quay, was councillor Sharley who was in office from 1942-1944. The shot itself dates from 1943. The 'Specials' to his left and the soldiers (both British and American) with the backdrop of the military vehicles suggests some sort of special wartime event. The absence of civilian vehicles is not unexpected given the severe rationing of petrol then in operation. To the right of the Mayor is Mr.Backway the town clerk whilst the macebearer on the left is Mr.Beer - and between the Mayor and the macebearer is the Reverend Mr.Muller.

119

Following the Second World War Britain entered the 'Cold War' with the Communist bloc in Eastern Europe. As part of the country's preparations for a war, which thankfully never came, a Civil Defence Corps was set up. Bideford members practised in the specially designed building known as 'The Folly'. Here we see Corps members lowering a stretcher case down a ladder. As the threat from the East receded so Civil Defence declined and eventually disappeared.

Above: On VE Day (Victory in Europe, 7-8 May 1945) - the children of the town were treated to free rides on the many small naval craft then in the Torridge. This photograph shows two of the vessels packed with children (and their mothers) taking advantage of the offer.

Overleaf: In the months following the end of the Second World War many celebratory street parties were held around Bideford. This shot shows the one put on in Royston Road where the excited children are flanked by their proud mothers - note the absence of men - they were still to be 'demobilised'.

Sport

Above: This marvellous display of beards, moustaches and headgear belonged to the members of the Bideford Bowling Club sometime around 1895. At various times the club ground was in Chingswell Street (on the opposite side to where it is today) and also for a while on the site of today's police station.

Overleaf: Could any photographer today get everyone in such a large crowd to pose for them in the way this one did? This group shot, taken outside the Royal Hotel shows a 'meet' of the Honourable Mark Rolle's Fox Hounds sometime around 1902-3. Note the ornate canopy over the steps up to the station which seem to be in the process of construction.

J. SHORTRIDGE. C. CROSSMAN (Stroke). R. W. MURPHY (Trainer). H. B. HOOKWAY. W. A. SANDERS.
H. HOPKINS (Cox.)

Bideford's two rowing clubs have a long and proud history and luckily they have given rise to many photographic mementoes over the years. This particular one shows the Bideford Amateur Athletics crew of 1898 standing stiffly behind their cups and medals. The rather incongruous backdrop was a studio prop used by the photographer W.H.Puddicombe at his premises in the Strand.

BIDEFORD
REGATTA
PONY RACES & SPORTS,
Monday, Aug. 24th, 1896.

SPORTS will commence about 11.30 a.m. with DUCK HUNTS in Bridge Pool.

PROGRAMME OF RACES ON THE SANDS.

PONIES not exceeding 12½ h.h. 1st Prize, £1 10s.; 2nd, 15s.; 3rd, Pair Nickel-Plated Spurs.

PONIES not exceeding 13½ h.h. 1st Prize, £2; 2nd, £1; 3rd, Riding Whip, presented by Mr. George Tucker.

GALLOWAYS not exceeding 14½ h.h. 1st Prize, £2; 2nd, value £1; 3rd, Breeches, presented by Mr. Frank Trapnell.

STEEPLE CHASE for Horses not exceeding 14½ h.h., over Water and Hurdles. First Prize, £2; 2nd, £1; 3rd, 10s.

CONSOLATION RACE. 1st Prize, Silver-Plated Tankard, presented by Mr. W. H. Jewell; 2nd, Boots, presented by Mr. W. Hodge; 3rd, Whip.

DONKEY RACE. 1st Prize, Bridle, presented by Mr. T. Pridham; 2nd, Hat, presented by Mr. G. H. Andrew; 3rd, Set Jugs, presented by Mr. Sharp.

FOOT RACING FOR MEN. 1 Mile. Open. 1st Prize, Set Carvers, presented by the Sunlight Soap Company; 2nd Clock, presented by Mr. E. Northwood; 3rd, Hat, presented by Mr. A. E. J. Child.

LAND-AND-WATER RACE. First Prize, Silver-Plated Cup, presented by Mr. Alfred Oatway; 2nd, Pair Shoes, presented by the Public Benefit Boot Company; 3rd, Handsome Pocket Knife.

QUARTER-MILE RACE for BOYS under 14. 1st Prize, Watch and Chain, presented by Mr. E. Grimes; 2nd 1 dozen Plated Tea Spoons, presented by Mr. P. H. Jenkin; 3rd, Pair Vases, presented by Mrs. Bale.

SWIMMING RACE for BOYS under 16. Its prize Clock, pres by Messrs. Squire and Son; 2nd Gold Scarf Pin, presented by Mr. H. M. Prow.

Any Pony that has won Three First Racing Prizes to be ineligible for either of the above Races.

All Ponies will be Measured in Brunswick Yard, East-the-Water, before the Races, at 10.30 a.m.

Entrance Fee for Ponies, 2s.6d.; all the rest, Free. All Entries to be made in Writing, and RACING COLOURS named, to the Honorary Secretary, not later than FRIDAY EVENING, the 21st August, 1896.

All Disputes to be settled by the Committee, whose decision shall be final, and subject to no appeal in any Court of Law.

July, 1896.

W. B. JOHNS, HON. SEC.

Bideford Regatta has a long history in the town but hasn't always been focused on rowing. On another page I have shown a photograph of the Sports Day associated with the event but this 1896 poster advertises various other events including horse racing which took place on the sand banks exposed at low tide in the Torridge.

Above: Bideford has long been famous for its two rowing clubs whose members have won many victories over the years. Such clubs, however, need new boats every now and again and this photograph shows one such boat being formally presented in May 1957. In this case it had been paid for by H.W.Fulford and was going to the Bideford Amateur Rowing Club. Here we see the benefactor's daughter Miss Winsome Fulford breaking a bottle of something over the bows of the boat. Standing either side of her are Frank Day, a former club treasurer, and C.J.Mitchell, a life member of the club.

Above: Bideford Regatta sees teams of ultra fit young people converge on the town annually to compete for the rowing cups on offer. In September 1979, however, the Bideford Reds' Veteran crew pictured here won the Veteran's Race. The team consisted of (left to right) David Hutchings, Ken Drew, Ken Hearn and Terry Palmer, with David's son Steve as coxswain. The four had an overall age of 159 between them and had been rowing for a cumulative total of some 93 years!

Opposite page: Another shot of one of the rowing club teams who, having just carried their boat down the old gig steps by the Kingsley Statue have launched it into the Torridge - and paused just long enough to have their photograph taken from a boat in the river. Note the cameraman on the left with his unwieldy looking tripod and glass plate camera - digital technology has made it all so much easier.

129

Bideford Regatta is now built around the races on the river but in the 1960s the Sports Day was also a notable event. Even in 1968 when this photo was taken the organisers were bemoaning the lack of participating teams. Apathy might have been creeping in but this photo shows that the races that took place were exciting. The winner of this particular race, the 660 yards, was P.Brown from the Queen's Park Harriers.

Above: The Bideford Bowling Club was established in 1889 and over the years many thousands of games have been staged there - including this one in August 1969. The photograph recording the event shows Archie Thorne in action during the county fours final. The bulk of the Strand Cinema, now replaced by Strand Court, is in the background to the left.

Overleaf: Boys of the Old Town swimming club pictured in 1921 - all wearing a rather unwieldy looking swimming costume. The school burnt down in 1926 and today the site is occupied by the fire station. One wonders where the boys actually swam as there was no swimming pool in the town - so either they used the river or, less likely given the distance involved, the sea.

Old Town School
Bideford
Swimmers
1921

Amongst the usual range of sports clubs in the town Bideford is the Rifle Club. In February 1964 they were competing in the Devon and Cornwall Rifle League and some of the members are shown in this photograph though I am unsure as to where they met to shoot.

Above: This fascinating, though technically poor shot, shows the Sports Ground sometime before 1927 (Kingsley Road has yet to be built) with a game of football going on. The bowling green is in the foreground - with nets around it to presumably protect it from over-enthusiastic footballers. Note the shippen on the right - which stood roughly where the bridge into Morrison's car park now stands.

Opposite: Although the Bideford Amateur Athletics Club is probably best known for its rowing teams it has also fostered a number of football teams over the years. This team from 1931-32 was captured at the Sports Ground. Note their trainer's 'Gladstone' bag on the ground at the right.

Bideford A.A.C. 1931 - 32.

In November 1970 the Bideford 'Robins' Football Team were riding high on top of the Western League when disaster struck. Centre-forward Russell Petersen was playing for the team when he broke his leg and had to be stretchered off - but what made it even worse was that only 24 hours later the club's manager Graham Bond (right foreground in picture) when playing in a Reserves' game also broke his leg! Not a good time for the Robins.

Entertainment

Above: Bideford Carnival used to be held specifically to raise funds for the Hospital - at a time when it was supported by charitable donations and community effort. This wonderful looking group of young women and a 'Native American' seem to be part of a group pushing the barrel organ/piano outside of what today is Mr.Chips.

Overleaf: Today Bideford Carnival consists of a mix of walking characters interspersed with lorries and other motor vehicles. This photograph, which is thought to date from the inter-war years, shows how things used to be done. The patient horse is pulling what, to modern eyes, is a rather basic looking kitchen - note the two mangles on the left and the wooden ironing board - though I suspect this might be a spoof tableaux. Taken on the Pill facing Charles Avenue it shows, if nothing else, how the Carnival has changed.

In May 1935 Bideford staged a 'Rainbow Pageant' at the Sports Ground when local schoolchildren dressed in a variety of different coloured clothes to represent the countries making up the British Empire. This group were the 'Atlantic Islands' - which presumably included Bermuda, Ascension Island, St.Helena, Tristan da Cunha and the Falklands. Elliott's garage is in the background.

On page 40 of 'Illustrations of Old Bideford' I published a photograph of the old Garden Theatre on the Pill which was built in the 1930s and which saw some of the first appearances of Paul Scofield in the war years. This is what he would have seen from the stage - a very basic looking auditorium though the plentiful use of wooden planking on the walls must have helped with the acoustic properties of the hall.

Bideford Carnival has always been an important event in the town's calendar and in the past many local stores actively encouraged their staff to prepare entries and foremost amongst them was Chopes. Their 'girls' often produced very inventive groups based on a shared theme - as shown in this photograph. It captures a group dressed as human 'powder puffs' pictured on the Pill. Such cleverness often won them prizes - and quite rightly so considering the amount of work that must have gone into preparing their costumes.

Another firm who encouraged their staff to enter the 'group' section of the Carnival were Heywood & Cock whose drapery shop was at the top of Grenville Street. This photograph showing a very inventive theme dates from September 1936 when the Carnival was still one of the main fund-raisers for the town's Hospital. I can only identify one person in the shot - the lady in glasses was Ethel Ley.

I couldn't resist this photograph which shows Bideford schoolboys watching a 'magic' show at the Bideford Church Institute in the early 1950s. The shorts, ties and haircuts couldn't really be from any other period. The lad in the long trousers is Roger Hopkins and next to him on the left is Roy Hopkins whilst the boy with his hand up to his face is Peter Watts. Innocent times.

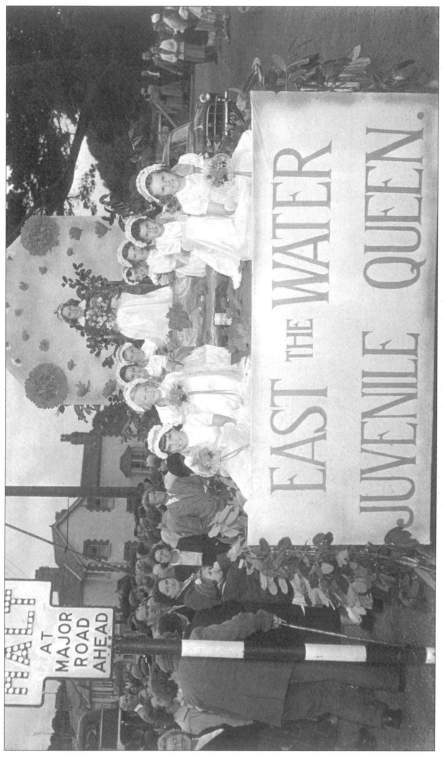

This is one of the nicest Carnival photographs in my possession. It dates from August 1956 and shows the East-the-Water Queen - 11 year old Angela Vanstone with her attendants who included Margaret Day, Gillian Pope, Hazel Thomas, Angela Mitchell, Valerie Steer and Joy Young all of whom had been elected by popular vote the month before.

Above: This happy looking group were photographed mid-dance in the Bideford Rugby Club hut (evidently an old Nissen hut by the look of it) in February 1957. The event was a Young Conservatives Rag Dance - though I always thought Rag days were connected with schools and colleges but there we are. The lad with the superb quiff wearing a uniform in the middle is a member of the Royal Observer Corps.

Overleaf: Not a contortionist's act - but rather one of the party games played at the annual dinner of the Bideford branch of the Royal Observer Corps held in the New Inn in the town in 1959. The Corps had been the 'eyes and ears' of the RAF during the Second World War and it continued in existence until 1991. Following the war its function had changed slightly to monitoring Russian aircraft flying over British air space - a role made redundant by the ever increasing sophistication of radar. Its last job was to have been observing the effects of a nuclear attack on Britain.

This smiling group of young dancers were members of the Strand School of Dancing run by Miss Teresa Smith. In March 1970 she had arranged and choreographed a show entitled 'Studio 70' with all the proceeds going to the Taw and Torridge Society for the Mentally Handicapped. Putting the show together with so many young people must have taken some organisation.

In the early 1970s Bideford had a zoo just past Ford House and here we see the arrival of Elsa a 7 year-old Asiatic elephant in June 1972. Elsa had a rheumatism related illness in her front leg but careful nursing saved her from being put down at the unnamed European zoo where she was then living. Her owners presented her to Bob Howard the proprietor of Bideford zoo and she became a popular resident at his concern. The zoo itself is long gone and the site now hosts a housing estate - but I wonder what happened to Elsa?

148

Miscellaneous

This photograph wasn't actually taken in Bideford but it does show the members of the Bideford Young Men's Christian Association on a Good Friday outing to Peppercombe beach. Most of the members seem to be in the band - and I cannot recall seeing many marching bands with three violins amongst their ranks!

This studio photograph dates from around 1866 and shows Kate Bazeley one of the four daughters of Bideford's then vicar the Reverend F.L.Bazeley. Kate who had been born in Plymouth around 1845 was then a young woman at the height of contemporary fashion when she went along to the studio of George Hopson in Mill Street for this portrait.

This shot dates from 1866 and was taken by George Hopson of Mill Street. It is untitled but appears to show a churchwarden - an officer of the church who was responsible for keeping the ecclesiastical buildings in good order. It came from a collection of photographs belonging to the Reverend F.L. Bazeley and his family so it probably commemorates one of St.Mary's churchwardens.

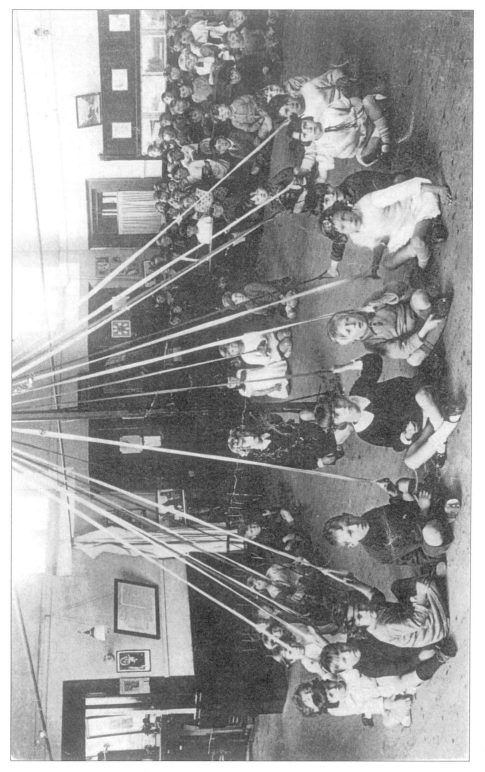

This charming photograph dates from the 1920s and shows the Sunday School pupils of the East-the-Water Bethel. They are obviously engaged in a May Pole dance - which had only been re-introduced in North Devon some 50 years before - it being regarded, quite rightly, as a 'pagan' dance. How times change.

The Bideford Band has been photographed many times over the years as it has appeared at so many public occasions. Here they are seen in the 1930s on the Quay. The bandmaster on the right is Joe Heal, next to him with a tuba is Kingsley Hearn and behind is Bert Cole. The man with the trombone is George Branch and the lady on the left in glasses looking at the camera is Maud Cole - with Walter Cole behind her in flat cap.

I do not know why this group was assembled but it shows residents of Brookfield Street, East-the-Water probably in the late 1930s/early 1940s. I have included it as it shows Bidefordians in their everyday clothes - including the various workaday 'pinnies' being worn by the women.

Bideford Co., C. L. B.—Holders of both Challenge Cups, 1907

The title to this group is self-explanatory - and if you don't know what 'CLB' stands for it is the Church Lads Brigade. This was a Christian youth group roughly based on a military set-up - indeed note the rifles held at the slope by the boys in the back row. Many if not most of these lads would have fought in the First World War - then only 7 years away.

This cheerful looking celebration was a street party in New Street staged to mark the Silver Jubilee of George V in 1935. All of these houses have now gone - demolished over 40 years ago and replaced (eventually!) by new flats on the left hand side with the area on the right providing car parking and rear servicing to shops in Mill Street.

This packed photograph shows the crowds who turned out in Bideford to mark George VI's Coronation Day in 1937. Note Braddick's loudspeaker van in the background and the wide variety of headgear on display. I am personally always intrigued by the numbers on these photographs - this was No.11 yet it is the only one from this series I have seen.

Photographs of the Bideford Sea Cadets often turn up as they have been present, at many of the town's public 'events' since the Second World War. This more informal shot dates from around 1960 and shows three of the adult officers; from left to right they are, Sub-Lieutenant Walter Chubb, Lieutenant Commander T.N.Rowe and Lieutenant Bridger

Above: One of Britain's best supported charities is that supplying Guide Dogs for the Blind and this photograph from June 1957 shows a novel fund raising event in Bideford's Jubilee Square. Those taking part paid 1/- (5p) each to write their name on a label attached to a helium filled balloon. These were then released the winner being the person whose label was returned to the organisers from the furthest distance away. The organisers were trying to raise £250 which equates to some 5000 balloons - I wonder if they made it?

Overleaf: Bideford Fire Brigade can trace its origins back to 1770 when the Bridge Trust purchased a hand-pumped fire engine with leather pipes which was stored under the Town Hall. Since then the town has had a volunteer fire brigade in some form - including the men shown here in a photograph dating from 1959. They were back row (left to right), Ted Webb, Ivor Shortridge, Reg Balls, Ron Hammett; middle row, Louis Rowson, Tom Glover, Ivor Giddy, Clifford Coates, Louis Violet, Graham Cole, Jack Heywood, Alan Percicole; front row, Kingsley Hearn, Tom Trick, Fred Tithecott, Bill Nichols, Jack Mallett.

Clearly this is Victoria Park but what was ambulance doing there? In 1975 the Bideford Rotary Club celebrated its 50th birthday by presenting a £5000 fully equipped emergency vehicle to the town's St.John Ambulance unit. Some £99 of the cost came from the Rotary Club in Uelzen, Bideford's German 'friendship' town. The photograph shows Ron Smith the President of Bideford Rotary handing over the keys of the ambulance to the Superintendent of St.John Ambulance John Brown.

Above: Bideford is a generally quiet town but in August 1975 an Essex man came to see relatives in the area following his marriage breakdown and, after obtaining a shotgun, went to the Royal Mail Inn at the bottom of Bridge Street where he ordered all the staff and customers to leave. The police quickly arrived and Chief Inspector John Edwards attempted to defuse the situation by talking to him. Sadly he was unsuccessful and the man committed suicide. The photograph shows the police operation going on.

Opposite: I have included this shot as it shows one of the least photographed yet most fascinating streets in Bideford - Coldharbour. No-one knows the true derivation of the name which is common throughout Britain but we do know that this steep and winding street marked the edge of Bideford right up until the end of the nineteenth century. This shot was taken in June 1977 and shows the street party held to mark the Queen's Silver Jubilee - one of the many which took place all over Bideford.

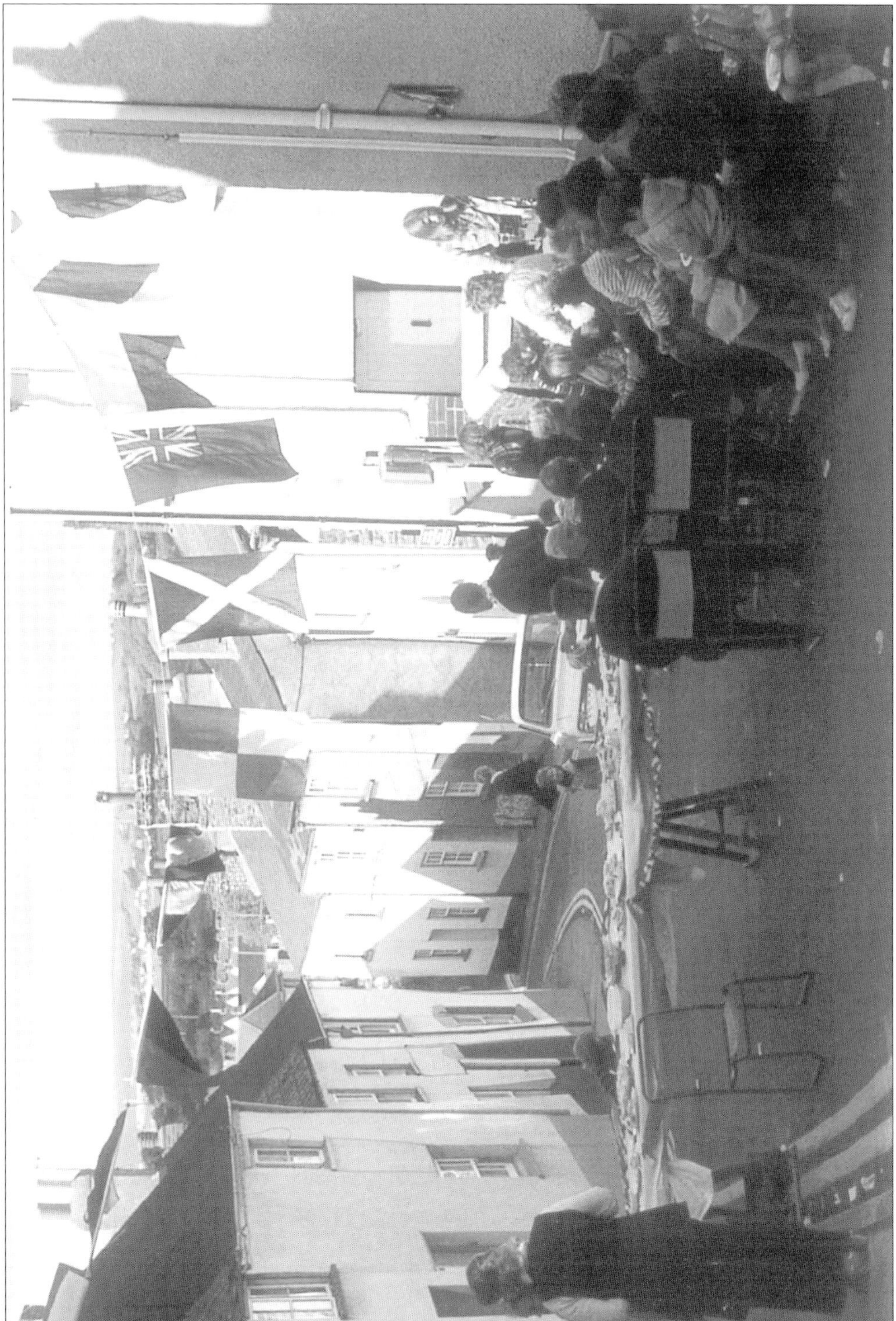

These were the Bideford Girl Guides and Brownies pictured in March 1981 when they were visited by the Honourable Mrs. Gervase Clay, the daughter of Lady Baden-Powell, and South West President of the Girl Guides. The group was pictured in their old headquarters which used to stand behind the tennis courts at the Sports Ground.

Every year the town council, working in conjunction with local shopkeepers, has erected Christmas lights around the town - and every year the lights have steadily grown in size and ornateness. If you don't believe me look at this display from 1990. It also gives a snapshot of the High Street some 20 years ago - with a charity shop where Ladbroke's now is in the building that was once Bideford's Post Office.

These people were members of the Geneva Revels amateur dramatic group, pictured around 1943. They took their name from Geneva School and were: Back row, left to right: Roy Dyer, Joyce Hancock, Tony Lloyd, Trudy Higgins, Dick Halbert, Joyce Webb, Tommy McCarthy, Barbara Harding. Front row: Ruby Lester, Margie Webb, C Harding, Helma Elliott, ? Beer.

In February 1984 Prince Charles visited North Devon and here we see him greeting some of the huge crowd who turned out to see him.

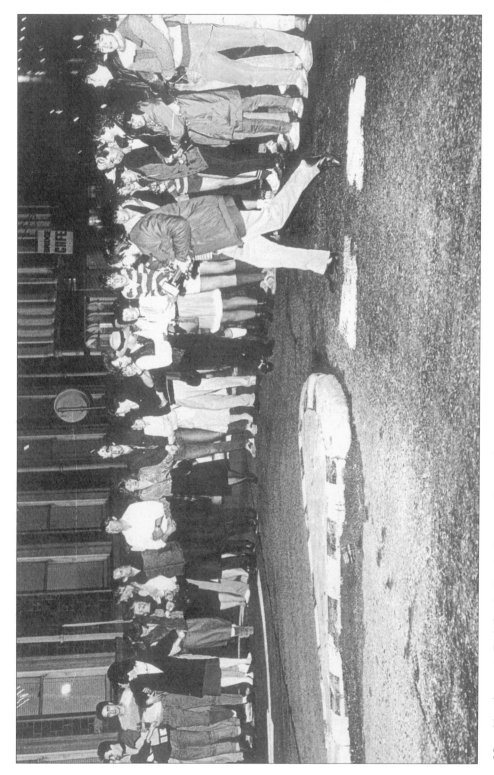

New Year's eve in Bideford attracts thousands - yet here we see a much smaller affair. It dates from 1984, and notice how few of the revellers are in the now almost obligatory fancy-dress.